Raintree
Publishers

Westlake M
Media Cer
2800 West
Broomfield,

369715

M000305225

DATE DUE

DEMCO 38-296

Westlake Middle School
Media Center
2800 West 135th Avenue
Broomfield, CO 80020

WORLD IN VIEW
ECUADOR, PERU, AND BOLIVIA
Marion Morrison

RAINTREE
STECK-VAUGHN
L I B R A R Y
The Steck-Vaughn Company
Austin, Texas

© Copyright 1992, text, Steck-Vaughn Company

All rights reserved. No reproduction, copy or transmission of this publication may be made without written permission from the publisher.

Library of Congress Cataloging-in-Publication Data

Morrison, Marion.
    Ecuador, Peru, and Bolivia / Marion Morrison.
       p.   cm.—(World in view)
    Includes index.
    Summary: Surveys the history, climate, geography, culture, religion, and economics of the three Andean countries of South America.
    ISBN 0-8114-2453-7
    1. Andes Region—Juvenile literature. [1. Andes Region.]
    I. Title. II. Series.
F2212.M67   1992   91-44980
980—dc20   CIP AC

Cover: *Aymara Indian on totora reed boat, Lake Titicaca, Bolivia*
Title page: *The village of Maras in the Eastern Cordillera of the Peruvian Andes*

Design by Julian Holland Publishing Ltd.

Consultant: Bruce Taylor, University of Dayton

Typeset by Multifacit Graphics, Keyport, NJ
Printed and bound in the United States
by Lake Book, Melrose Park, IL
1 2 3 4 5 6 7 8 9 0 LB 96 95 94 93 92

Photographic credits
All photographs supplied by South American Pictures:
Cover: Kimball Morrison/South American Pictues; 8, 66 Hilary Bradt, 26, 53, 92 Marion Morrison; 36, 52 Edward Parker; all remaining photographs by Tony Morrison.

Contents

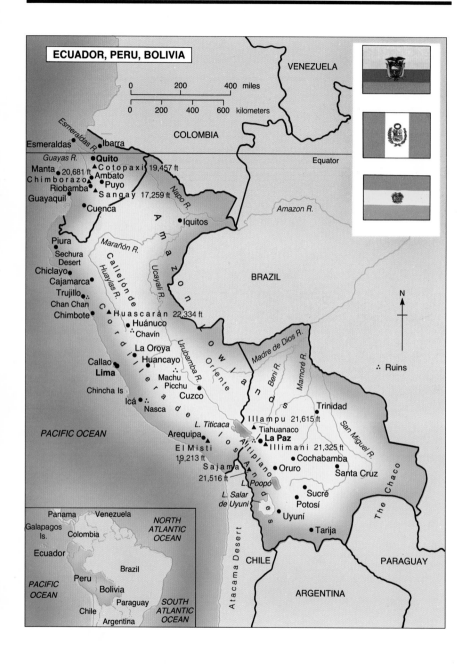

ECUADOR, PERU, BOLIVIA

0   200   400 miles

0   200   400   600 kilometers

VENEZUELA

COLOMBIA

Esmeraldas

Esmeraldas R.

Ibarra

Guayas R.

Quito

Manta ● 20,681 ft ▲ C o t o p a x i 19,457 ft

C h i m b o r a z o ● Ambato

Riobamba ● ● Puyo

Guayaquil ▲ S a n g a y 17,259 ft

● Cuenca

Equator

Napo R.

● Iquitos

Amazon R.

Piura

Marañón R.

Sechura
Desert

C a l l e j ó n d e

Chiclayo ●

Cajamarca ●

Huaylas R.

Ucayali R.

BRAZIL

Trujillo ●

Chan Chan

Chimbote ● ▲ H u a s c a r á n 22,334 ft

C
o
r
d
i
l
l
e
r
a

● Huánuco

∴ Chavín

La Oroya

Urubamba R.

Madre de Dios R.

Beni R.

Mamoré R.

Callao ● ● Huancayo

Lima

L
o
w
l
a
n
d
s

O
r
i
e
n
t
e

∴ Ruins

Chincha Is

∴ Machu
Picchu

d
e

● Cuzco

N

Icá ∴
● Nasca

l
o
s

Trinidad

L. Titicaca

I l l a m p u 21,615 ft

Arequipa ●

A
n
d
e
s

▲ Tiahuanaco

La Paz ●

San Miguel R.

PACIFIC OCEAN

E l M i s t i
19,213 ft

▲

Altiplano

▲ I l l i m a n i 21,325 ft

● Cochabamba

T
h
e

C
h
a
c
o

S a j a m a
21,516 ft

▲ ● Oruro

● Santa Cruz

L. Poopó

*L. Salar
de Uyuni*

● Sucré
● Potosí

● Uyuní

● Tarija

Panama   Venezuela

Galapagos
Is.   Colombia

NORTH
ATLANTIC
OCEAN

A
t
a
c
a
m
a

D
e
s
e
r
t

CHILE

PARAGUAY

Ecuador

Brazil

Peru

PACIFIC
OCEAN

Bolivia

Paraguay

SOUTH
ATLANTIC
OCEAN

Chile

Argentina

ARGENTINA

1

Three Andean Countries

The Andes Mountains run down the west side of South America. They extend from the Caribbean shores of Venezuela and Colombia in the north to the tip of Chile and the icy waters of the Antarctic in the far south. The countries of Ecuador, Peru, and Bolivia are in the central part of the range.

Ecuador is the smallest country of the three and

Fact Box

Ecuador
Capital Quito
Area 104,506 square miles
(270,670 square kilometers)
Population 10.5 million
Language Spanish
Currency Sucre = 100 centavos

Peru
Capital Lima
Area 496,222 square miles
(1,285,216 square kilometers)
Population 21.3 million
Language Spanish, Aymara, and Quechua
Currency New sol = 100 centavos

Bolivia
Capital La Paz
Area 424,164 square miles
(1,098,587 square kilometers)
Population 7.0 million
Language Spanish, Quechua, and Aymara
Currency Peso = 100 centavos

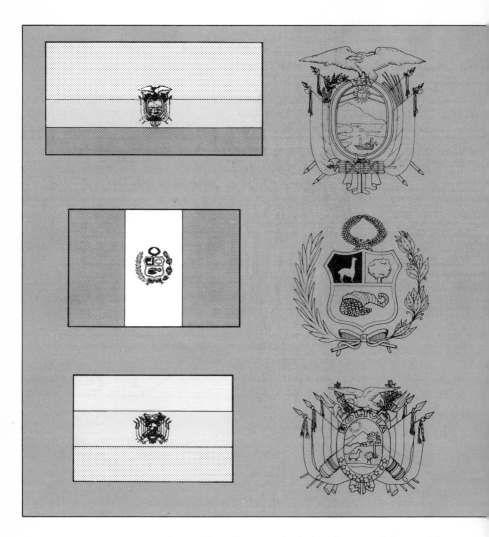

shares borders with Colombia and Peru. The equator crosses Ecuador, and this is what gives it its name. Its capital, Quito, is in the mountains, just south of the equator.

Peru is the largest of the three countries and is

Ecuador's Flag

This has horizontal stripes of yellow, blue, and red. These are the colors of the Republic of Gran Colombia to which Ecuador belonged until 1830. The coat of arms in the middle of the flag shows a condor (the national bird), Mount Chimborazo, which at 20,681 feet (6,310 meters) is the highest mountain in Ecuador, and a steamer on a lake.

Peru's Flag

This has vertical red and white stripes. The national emblem in the middle shows a horn of plenty, full of gold coins in the lower half. The upper half is divided in two with a golden llama in one part and in the other a leafy cinchona tree, from the bark of which come quinine and other powerful medicines.

Bolivia's State Flag

This has horizontal stripes of red, yellow, and green. The coat of arms shows a breadfruit tree, a sheaf of grain, a mountain, an alpaca, and a condor. The state flag is used in Bolivia by the government. The country's national flag has no coat of arms.

the third largest in South America after Brazil and Argentina. Peru shares a long border to the east with Brazil. To the south, it borders Bolivia and Chile. Both Ecuador and Peru have a coast on the Pacific Ocean, and Peru's capital, Lima, lies in the

Mount Illiniza 17,405 feet (5,305 meters) is one of several extinct snowcapped volcanoes close to the equator in Ecuador.

country's important coastal region.

Bolivia and Paraguay are the two South American countries with no coastline. However, Paraguay's rivers drain into the Plate River and the Atlantic whereas Bolivia has no access to the ocean. The Andes Mountains are at their widest in Bolivia, and La Paz, at 11,929 feet (3,636 meters), is the highest capital city in the world.

In all three countries most of the people live either in the mountains or on the coast. To the east of the mountains lies the Oriente, a vast region of Amazon lowlands where very few people live.

The mountains
In places the Andean chain is divided into two ranges known as the Eastern and Western

8

Cordilleras. The Eastern Cordillera has many of the highest mountains, which are snow-covered all year round. Peru has more than 10 peaks of over 19,685 feet (6,000 meters) with Husacarán, the highest, at 22,334 feet (6,768 meters). Husacarán and nearby Mount Huandoy attract mountaineers from all over the world. Both tower over a beautiful valley, the Callejón de Huaylas,

The Bolivian capital city, La Paz, was founded by the Spaniard Alfonso de Mendoza in 1548 in a deep valley at the base of Mount Illimani.

which has been the site of several disastrous earthquakes this century.

One of the most spectacular sections of the Eastern Cordillera is in Bolivia, close to La Paz. The city lies in a deep canyon at the foot of Mount Illimani, a magnificent peak, which is much revered in local folklore. Legends surround many of the mountains in this range. Mount Illampu, the name of the highest peak, means "god of storms," and the only flat-topped mountain, Mururata, lost its peak, people say, because an Andean god tried to knock the devil from its top.

The Western Cordillera of the Andes is younger and of volcanic origin. There are volcanoes in all three countries, but the Avenue of Volcanoes in Ecuador is famous. In it are more than 20 peaks of between 14,000 feet (4,267 meters) and 20,013 feet (6,100 meters), and these include Cotopaxi, which at 19,457 feet (5,896 meters) is among the world's highest active volcanoes. Here, too, is Sangay, one of the most active volcanoes. Fumes continually pour from its cone, and at night the glow from its red lava can be seen for many miles around.

The plateaus

In Ecuador a plain runs between the Cordilleras, and much of it is covered by high-altitude mountain vegetation called *paramo*. Hills cross the plain and between them are fertile valleys drained by many rivers. In Peru the valleys are at a higher altitude and the soil not so good. The whole of the mountain region in Ecuador and Peru is known locally as the *Sierra*.

Starting in the south of Peru and extending

A Yura Indian from southern Bolivia crossing a desolate high plain in the Eastern Cordillera of the Andes.

through much of Bolivia is the plain known as the Altiplano. It is much higher than the plain in Ecuador, averaging some 12,007 feet (3,658 meters) above sea level. Life on the Altiplano is very severe. There are few rivers and little rain. It seldom snows. Strong winds blow from the south, and the temperature changes from very hot during the day to well below freezing at night. There are few trees and little wildlife. Much of the plain is covered in spiky tough grasses, such as *ichu,* and scrub, called *tola,* which the highland people use as fuel. A high proportion of these people are Quechua and Aymara Indians.

At the southern end of the Altiplano, there are several dried salt lakes, or *salares,* formed because the Altiplano has no river drainage and water

High in the Andes Mountains, the Bolivian Indians scrape salt from the Salar de Uyuni, the world's largest salt flat. Each year the salt pan floods with water from nearby hills.

evaporates in the dry atmosphere leaving the salt crystals behind. One of these lakes, the Salar de Uyuni, is the largest salt flat in the world. In this shimmering expanse of whiteness, nothing lives or grows though people from nearby villages cut the salt and sell it in other parts of the country.

Lake Titicaca

At the northern end of the Altiplano lies Lake Titicaca, which spans the border between Peru and Bolivia. It is the highest lake in the world that large boats can sail across. Steam ferries were used from the end of the nineteenth century. Now a twice-weekly hydrofoil service travels across it. Most of the lake is in Peru, and it covers an area of 3,500 square miles (9,062 square kilometers). This great expanse of water looks like an inland sea with the snowcapped peaks of the Cordilleras just visible on the horizon.

For many centuries the Aymara Indians who live near the lake have depended on it for their living. The Indians have always used the *totora* reed that grows along the shore for building their boats and for the roofs of their houses. The reed is now also used commercially for matting, and there is a fear that the supply is being used up too quickly. This would pose a real threat to the many birds, such as reed birds, grebes, and ibis, which live in the totora. One species, the flightless grebe, lives only on Lake Titicaca. Within its deep, cold waters the lake still has many secrets. A few years ago the French diver, Jacques Cousteau, rediscovered a species of Titicaca frog, said to be

Aymara Indians living on the shores of Lake Titicaca fish from their totora reed boats. The reed grows in the lake. The snowcapped peaks of the Eastern Cordillera can be seen across the lake.

13

one of the largest in the world and thought to be extinct. Other expeditions have searched the lake for the remains of ancient cities and lost treasure. Some people believe the lake even has a legendary monster.

The eastern slopes

The eastern slopes of the Andes in Peru and Bolivia are the most fertile regions of both countries. From the high, snowcapped Cordilleras to the Amazon lowlands below, there is a very steep drop, and as the land falls away, the vegetation changes.

Below the snow line, the forested mountain slopes are wrapped in clouds for much of the year. The forest is full of trees covered with bromeliads, ferns often taller than a grown man, and many

The heavy rainfall in the Andes Mountains sends rivers tumbling eastward to the Amazon. These falls on the Coca River in Ecuador flow directly to the rain forest.

species of flowers, including passionflowers and orchids. Streams from the snows and waterfalls tumble over rocks everywhere.

At an altitude of about 9,000 feet (2,743 meters), the clouds and mist lift, and below the forest there are cultivated slopes where many people have small farms. The land is good for many crops, and, in recent years, there has been intensive cultivation of the coca plant. The plant's leaves are used to make cocaine. Many varieties of trees prized by the timber trade also grow on these lower slopes. The land is very fertile; however, access to the region remains difficult because there are so few roads.

The Oriente

The Amazon lowlands that extend east from the foothills of the Andes are called the Oriente. In Ecuador the Oriente covers one third of the country, and in Peru and Bolivia, two thirds.

It is a land of swamps, forests, and scrub grasslands, inhabited by only a few groups of forest Indians. Many rivers, making their way down the Andes, flow into the tributaries of the Amazon River. These tributaries run for hundreds of miles toward the mouth of the Amazon on the east side of the continent. From time to time, governments have introduced plans to persuade people to settle in the region. Recently, however, commercial firms, drawn by the value of the land's timber, and settlers wanting to clear areas for developments have taken matters into their own hands. The result has been extensive, uncontrolled destruction of the forests. People and governments worldwide

Much of the Peruvian coast is pure desert. By contrast the sea is rich in fish, which attracts many species of birds, including skimmers, gulls, and gannets.

are concerned about this destruction and have called on local governments to stop it.

The coast

Along the northern part of Ecuador's coast, where the rains are heavy, there is tropical rain forest. Farther south, the climate gradually becomes drier until, in Peru, the coastal zone becomes true desert.

The coastal zones of Ecuador and Peru are of vital economic importance to both countries. More than 50 percent of Ecuador's population lives on the coast, particularly in the region around the country's main port, Guayaquil. Many crops are grown in this region. The many rivers that flow from the Andes to the Pacific irrigate the land, but when the rains are heavy, there is constant danger of flooding. Almost half of Peru's population lives in the coastal zone, too. Fewer rivers cross the Peruvian desert, but where they do, the oasis valleys are very fertile. Peruvian offshore waters are also rich in fish.

Climate

In these countries climate and temperature depend on altitude. Although all three countries are in the tropics, only the lowland Oriente regions have a true hot and humid tropical climate all year round. In the mountains there are extremes of cold and heat with occasional strong winds. The rainy season tends to fall between November and April, and the driest months are June to August. Quite often, however, mini rainy seasons change this pattern.

The coastal waters of Ecuador and Peru are surprisingly cold. Winds coming inshore are cooled over the sea, and fog banks develop. This means that for many months each year the Peruvian desert is covered by a heavy, dull mist. Normally it never rains, but there is one phenomenon that changes this pattern. It is called El Niño, the Christ Child, because it usually arrives around Christmas.

El Niño is a current of warm water, blown south from the equator into the cold waters off the coast of Ecuador and Peru. It causes the temperature of the sea to rise so that the fish migrate to colder waters and evaporation is so great that exceptionally heavy rains fall on the coastal strip. Severe Niños have been recorded only four or five times this century, most recently in late 1982.

Guayaquil had the heaviest rainfall ever recorded there. Landslides and floods destroyed crops and cattle, roads and bridges. Another town in Ecuador was completely cut off. Many people died, and thousands of houses were destroyed.

Natural paradise
The Galapagos Islands, also known as the Archipiélago de Colón, are 602 miles (970 kilometers) west of the Ecuador coast. An archipelago is a group of islands, and the Galapagos consist of six main islands and twelve small ones. Scientists believe the islands are the peaks of very large volcanoes, and fumes can sometimes be seen on some of the more active islands. The Galapagos, which take their name from the giant tortoises found there, are famous for their unique wildlife. Many species of fish,

Charles Darwin in South America
In 1831 Charles Darwin, then 22, sailed as a naturalist on the HMS *Beagle* to survey the wildlife of the west coast of South America and some Pacific islands. During his studies on the five-year voyage, he developed his theory that animals adapt to their environment in order to survive. This theory formed the basis of his book, *On the Origin of Species,* which he wrote some 20 years later. He argued that the world had not just been created in a few days but that man and animals had evolved over a long period of time. He drew his conclusions partly from the unique animal life of the Galapagos Islands, where he noticed how similar species living on different islands within the archipelago had developed in different ways.

plants, and reptiles are found only in the Galapagos. Over tens of thousands of years, the plants and animals have developed on the islands and adapted to the conditions there. Some of the most interesting animals are the giant tortoise, the marine iguana, which is the only seagoing lizard in the world, and the fur seal. Among the birds are albatross and gannets.

The rivers

Many of the rivers flowing into the immense Amazon have their source in the Andes of Ecuador, Peru, and Bolivia. Many of the tributaries are themselves great rivers, hundreds of miles long. As they make their way across the Amazon lowlands, they merge into one another. For example, the Marañón, possibly the Amazon's longest tributary, absorbs the Napo, which rises near the volcano Cotopaxi in Ecuador, and the Ucayali/Urubamba, which rises in the south of Peru.

Other rivers flow from the Andes to the Pacific, and the largest river system with an outlet to the coast is the Guayas in Ecuador, with Guayaquil as its port. Another important river flowing out to Ecuador's coast is the Esmeraldas.

Some of Bolivia's rivers flow into another of South America's great river systems, the Paraguay/Paraná, which emerges as the Plate River at Buenos Aires in Argentina.

Wildlife

With so many different environments in the three countries, it is not surprising that their animal and plant life is also extremely varied. Within the forest habitat of the Amazon lowlands and the eastern slopes of the Andes, familiar animals include monkeys, jaguars, pumas, oppossums, snakes, and caimans, South American crocodiles. But there are many more that are less well known. The largest mammal is the tapir, which can weigh up to 302 pounds (137 kilograms). It shares the forest and the rivers with the world's largest rodent, the capybara.

The forests vibrate with the sound of hundreds of species of birds. Some, like the colorful toucans, parrots, and macaws are easy to spot, but there are hummingbirds, herons, screamers, trumpeters, ibis, storks, and many more. High in the mountains, the black condor is a truly impressive sight as it circles against the deep blue Andean sky. The James' flamingo is very rare. It lives on the spectacular Laguna Colorada or Red Lake in the remote south of Bolivia at more than 14,000 feet (4,267 meters) above sea level.

In the highlands, the domesticated llamas and alpacas are used to carry loads and are also sheared for their wool. Belonging to the same family are the wild vicuña and the guanaco. The vicuña is the smallest member and very prized for

The Chincha Islands

Off the coast of Peru are the Chincha Islands, another paradise for naturalists. On the Chinchas are hundreds of thousands of seabirds, such as pelicans, cormorants, and gannets that, over the centuries, have left great piles of their droppings. These droppings, called guano, are a good fertilizer and very valuable commercially.

This giant Puya raimondii, the largest flower spike in the world, is a native of the central Andean uplands. The Puya is a bromeliad, or relative of the pineapple. It grows to a height of 23 feet (seven meters) and bears up to 8,000 individual flowers.

its soft, silklike, tawny coat. For many years, vicuñas were ruthlessly hunted and killed for their wool and by the 1960s were close to extinction. Fortunately, an animal reserve was created, poachers were severely punished, and the vicuñas have survived.

2   Early History

Scientists believe that people arrived in South America about 200,000 years ago. The first inhabitants probably came by way of the Bering Strait from Asia into North America sometime toward the end of the Ice Age. Another theory is that some may have sailed across the Pacific Ocean from Polynesia. By 9000 B.C. they had reached the Andes and the Altiplano. They lived by hunting large mammals, such as ground sloths and the wild ancestors of llamas and alpacas.

Llamas were domesticated long ago and have been used as beasts of burden by Andean Indians for more than a thousand years.

They also fished and gathered wild plants. Archaeologists have found stone tools and arrowheads used for hunting birds that date from this time.

As the centuries passed, the people learned to cultivate a few crops and domesticated the llama. They began to settle together in communities, gradually developing ways of irrigating the land. The range of crops they grew extended to include corn, potatoes, beans, peppers, and peanuts. They also cultivated cotton and used it for making fishing nets. As the food supply improved, the population began to increase.

By about 1000 B.C. two distinct ways of life had emerged, separating the peoples of the Amazon lowlands from those of the Andes Mountains and the coastal zone. In the Amazon forest, people settled close to the rivers, using dugout canoes to fish and hunt. Little has remained of these people's past because everything decayed so quickly in the tropical climate. Much more is known of the Andean peoples, particularly those living on the coast where the dry climate has preserved many sites and objects.

Pre-Columbian civilizations

Some of the oldest objects, including fine ceramic bowls, masks, and stone figures have been discovered on the coast of Ecuador, but the more advanced civilizations developed in Peru. Two of the earliest cultures appeared between 1200 B.C. and 1000 B.C. at Cerro Sechín on the coast and Chavín de Huantar in the mountains. Both produced stone sculpture, that of Cerro Sechín depicting human "trophy" heads and that of Chavín, catlike motifs. The Paracas culture of about 700 B.C. is famous for its weavings, discovered when archaeologists were excavating a burial site in the 1920s. The Nasca culture (500

B.C. to A.D. 600) is perhaps best known for some curious geometric designs and drawings of birds and fish, which were created in the desert. The designs spread over a vast area and can be seen most clearly from the air. The people made these huge shapes by removing the surface pebbles to expose the yellow sand underneath. The Nasca were also excellent potters.

The most skilled artisans were the Mochica, who lived from the time of Christ to about A.D. 600. Their center was at Moche, near present-day Trujillo, on the north coast of Peru, where they built the *Huaca del Sol*, or Pyramid of the Sun. This enormous mud pyramid is 131 feet (40 meters) high and about 492 feet (150 meters) long and took hundreds of years to build.

One great civilization developed on the Altiplano. Its people built a large ceremonial center at Tiahuanaco, just to the south of Lake Titicaca and more than 12,000 feet (3,657 meters) above sea level. It consisted of pyramids, temple platforms, and huge stone statues of gods. The Gateway to the Sun is most impressive with its carved frieze showing Viracocha, the god of creation. The gateway is carved from a single ten-ton block of gray volcanic rock called andesite.

The Tiahuanaco culture declined sometime after A.D. 1000, at which time another coastal civilization was developing. This was the Chimú kingdom, centered on the great city of Chan Chan. Chan Chan is a large walled compound made of mud that covers 2.32 square miles (6 square kilometers). Inside the compound were palaces, storerooms, and simple living accommodations. The Chimú were a very well-

The ruins of Chan Chan. The Chimú built this great city of mud bricks on the Peruvian coast, near the present-day city of Trujillo. The ruins are now being restored, and workmen are uncovering many fine mud decorations

369715

organized society with hereditary chiefs, noblemen, and commoners. Between the twelfth and fifteenth centuries, they established an empire that covered much of the northern coast of Peru. During the 1460s, however, they were conquered by an even more powerful civilization from the mountains, the Incas.

The Incas

In 1200 the Incas were one of a number of small tribes living in the Peruvian highlands near present-day Cuzco. For 200 years they developed gradually until in the second half of the fifteenth century, they began serious expansion of their empire under the ruler Inca Pachacuti. In about 50 years they conquered all of present-day Peru and

Westlake Middle School
Media Center
2800 West 135th Avenue
Broomfield, CO 80020

Machu Picchu, a fortified Incan town, lay hidden in a remote valley of the Peruvian Andes until 1911, when Hiram Bingham, an explorer from the United States, found it and named it "The Lost City of the Incas."

Bolivia, most of Ecuador, some of south Colombia, and a large part of Chile and northwest Argentina. They did not achieve this without considerable resistance from other local tribes, particularly the Colla and Lupaca of the present-day Bolivian Altiplano, and the Canaris and Shyris of Ecuador.

The Incas called their empire the *Tahuantinsuyu*, and it was divided into four quarters with the capital at Cuzco. Pachacuti was a capable administrator. He decreed that one Indian language, Quechua, should be used throughout the empire. When he conquered new territories, surveys were carried out to see if the land was good for crops or whether there were deposits of valuable minerals. If a workforce was needed in a different part of the empire or if there were troublemakers, sections of the population were moved. A count was made of all young men fit to join the Incan army.

Inca was the name given to the emperor and the nobles who administered the empire. The nobles became governors of newly won provinces and were helped by local chiefs called *curacas*. The rest of the people were commoners. They were organized into groups of families descended from a common ancestor. These groups were called *ayllus*. Within the *ayllu* each person had to work, usually on the land or at some craft.

There was a complex system of laws. Laws dictated what each household could own, and there were inspectors who checked regularly on hygiene and living standards. Crime was severely punished. Life was strictly organized, but everyone, even the sick and old, was taken care of by the state. For relaxation there were many feasts held to celebrate the farming seasons or in honor of the Incan emperor.

The weakness of the Inca empire was that it grew too big, too quickly. The Inca Huayna Capac made the last conquests in northern Ecuador and then lived in Quito until his death in 1526. He left the empire divided. His son, Huáscar, assumed control, but Huáscar's half brother, Atahualpa, challenged his authority. Civil war broke out. Huáscar was captured and later, on Atahualpa's orders, put to death. Atahualpa had just reached the town of Cajamarca on his way across the mountains from Quito to Cuzco when news reached him that strangers had landed on the coast. The Spaniards had arrived.

Discovery

In 1492 Christopher Colombus, leading an expedition for the king and queen of Spain, made his first voyage to the Americas and landed on some small islands in the Caribbean. He came closest to the South American mainland on his third voyage, in 1498, when he may have set foot on the north coast of Venezuela. News of his findings spread rapidly within Spain, and a number of explorers soon set sail for the New World in search of treasure. There were many stories of rich kingdoms that were full of gold.

In 1532 Francisco Pizarro, a Spanish soldier, reached Peru with fewer than 200 men. They made a decision to venture inland, a formidable journey over frozen mountain passes, where even the hardiest soldier would struggle in the thin air at more than 16,000 feet (4,877 meters) above sea level. They feared ambush from the natives, but, unknown to them, Atahualpa in Cajamarca had decreed that they be allowed to pass unhindered.

No one is sure why Atahualpa chose to make this decision, because he certainly had the means to stop the Spaniards, and if he had used those means the conquest that followed might never have taken place. Perhaps he was just curious, or perhaps he remembered an old Incan legend that predicted the return of the white, bearded gods of creation, whom the legend said had sailed away to the west many years before. The Spaniards were indeed white and bearded and came from the west. Not only that, but they rode horses, animals the Incas had never seen before.

Whatever the reason, Atahualpa agreed to

The keeper of the quipu. The quipu was the knotted string device used by the Incas for keeping records. The Incas had no form of writing.

Portraying the Incas
In the early seventeenth century the Indian writer Felipe Guaman Poma de Ayala produced the only pictorial account of Incan life. His monumental work is illustrated with more than 300 pen-and-ink drawings of daily life before and after the Spanish Conquest.

Guaman's drawings show various styles of dress. They show how the land was farmed, and portray the festivals related to the farming year. He drew the Incan emperors and nobles and men who held some of the important posts, such as the keeper of the quipu and the inspector of bridges.

His detailed work shows only too clearly the disastrous effect the Spanish Conquest had on the lives of the Indians as their way of life was destroyed by their new rulers.

meet the Spaniards, but the Europeans were now aware of the size and strength of the Inca empire and prepared an ambush for the emperor. Atahualpa was seized and many of his men killed. His life was ransomed for a vast amount of gold, which was collected from all corners of the empire. The Spaniards, however, executed Atahualpa anyway.

Cuzco fell easily to the conquerors, who, by 1534, had taken Quito as well. It took almost another 40 years for the Spaniards to put an end to Incan resistance. This resistance lost its focus with the death of the last Incan ruler, Tupac Amaru. Several of the leading Spanish conquerors had also been murdered or executed. Pizarro himself was assassinated in 1541.

Colonial life

To administer its new colonies, the Spanish Crown created viceroyalties, headed by a viceroy, who ruled with the help of a council or *audiencia*. The Spanish settlers, who were made up of the original soldiers, priests, and other newcomers out to seek their fortunes, took over much of the farming land and explored the region for gold and silver mines.

One discovery, in 1545, must have been beyond their wildest dreams. This was the Cerro Rico, or Rich Hill of Potosí in southern Bolivia. The Cerro Rico produced more silver than the world had ever known, and throughout the

The First Amazon Explorer

Francisco de Orellana was a Spanish soldier who took part in the conquest of Peru. In 1541 he prepared an expedition with Pizarro's half brother, Gonzalo, to explore the regions east of Quito in Ecuador. Orellana set off first with a group of 50 soldiers. They made their way down the mountains and into the lowlands, reaching the junction of the Napo and Marañón rivers, from which they realized there was no turning back. Instead, they continued exploring downstream, along the tributaries and down the Amazon itself. They eventually arrived at its mouth, on the Atlantic coast at the other side of the continent, 16 months later in August 1542. On his return to Spain, Orellana told of hoards of gold and quantities of spices and of encounters with tribes of women who reminded him of the Amazons in Greek mythology. It is believed that the river was called the Amazon after them.

From the Cerro Rico, *or Rich Hill, of Potosí in the Bolivian highlands, Spanish miners in the sixteenth and seventeenth centuries extracted more silver than the world had ever seen before.*

sixteenth and seventeenth centuries, this extraordinary wealth enriched the treasury of Spain. Potosí, cold, high, and inhospitable though it was, became the largest city in Spanish America, with a population at one time of 160,000. Charles V of Spain called it the "Imperial City," and its motto read, "I am rich Potosí, the treasure of the world and the envy of kings."

The riches of Potosí and other mines were extracted at a terrible cost to the local Indians. The Spanish forced them to work as slaves in the mines. In this they followed the Incan practice of making all males work several months of each year to fulfill the state labor obligation called the *mita*. Under Spanish rule, whole populations were moved to provide labor in the mines. Those

31

working on the land fared little better. Allotted to a particular settler, under a system known as the *encomienda*, they, too, lived and worked as slaves. Also, thousands of Indians died when they were exposed, for the first time, to European diseases and epidemics. As a result, there was often a shortage of labor, particularly in the mines and on the coastal plantations, so black slaves were brought from Africa and the Caribbean to do the work instead.

Among the Spanish settlers were Catholic priests and missionaries whose aim was to convert the local people. Some of them did what they could to help the Indians, but the Church mostly sided with the Creoles, Spaniards born in America, and kept a firm control over the people.

During the eighteenth century, the Creoles began to resent the Spanish rulers' stranglehold on the administrative and commercial life of the colonies. They were also aware that revolutionary movements were taking place in Europe. This, combined with the misery of the Indians and the discontent of the *mestizos*, people of mixed Indian and Spanish blood, led to many uprisings.

Struggle for independence

In 1808 Napoleon Bonaparte invaded Spain and deposed King Ferdinand VII. Many colonies in the New World saw this as their opportunity to break away from Spain, and in 1809 both present-day Ecuador and Bolivia declared their independence. The Spanish authorities and the *peninsulares*, Spaniards born in Spain but living in the colonies, fought back. Many years of struggle and turmoil followed.

The battle for independence in South America was led by Simón Bolívar, a Venezuelan, in the north, and José de San Martín, an Argentinian, in the south, San Martín's troops sailed from Chile in 1820 and landed in southern Peru and proclaimed independence in Lima in 1821 even though most of the country was still in royalist hands. Bolívar, who had already liberated

Simón Bolívar was a man with great vision. He led the fight for the independence of several colonies from Spain, and the Republic of Bolivia was named in his honor.

33

Venezuela and Colombia, sent his lieutenant, Antonio de José Sucre, into Ecuador. There, Sucre defeated the Spanish viceroy in the battle of Pichincha in 1822.

Bolívar was now able to create the first part of his dream of a United States of South America. He formed the Federation of Gran Colombia, made up of the present-day countries of Colombia, Panama, Venezuela, and Ecuador. A question mark, however, hung over the city of Guayaquil. Should it belong to Ecuador or Peru? A famous meeting was held in Guayaquil between Bolívar and San Martín, at the end of which San Martín left the campaign and went into self-imposed exile. Guayaquil became part of Ecuador.

Bolívar and Sucre were then free to help Peru with its struggle, and they won victories at the battles of Junín and Ayacucho in 1824. Sucre then moved into present-day Bolivia and secured its independence in the battle of Tumusla in 1825. It became a republic, governed by its own people or their elected representatives, and it was named Bolivia after Simón Bolívar.

3 The New Republics

Independence had been achieved, but for the ordinary people of Ecuador, Peru, and Bolivia, very little changed. They were free of Spain but still poor and without land. The large estates still belonged to Creoles, known locally as *criollos*, who, as wealthy landowners, had political power and control over the masses. A new kind of political leader emerged, the *caudillo* or strong man, often a war hero. Sometimes these war heroes and estate owners were liberals and other times they were conservatives, but they could always be greedy and ruthless.

The colonial years left the rich silver mines exhausted and the new republics with little to trade. The war of independence had caused devastation everywhere, and there were large debts to be paid. Years of turmoil and chaos followed, with many changes of leadership. It was always the poor, tied to the land, who suffered the most.

Ecuador

Ecuador emerged from the struggle as part of the Federation of Gran Colombia. It was only in 1830, when the Federation broke up, that Ecuador became a truly independent nation. General Juan José Flores was the caudillo who dominated Ecuador until he was overthrown in a revolution in 1845. After years of instability, Gabriel García Moreno became president in 1860, staying in office until 1865. He was also president from 1869 to 1875, when he was assassinated. García

Quito, the capital of Ecuador, lies in an Andean valley less than 19 miles (30 kilometers) south of the equator. It is a small city where the wealth from new business blends closely with a rich colonial past.

Moreno believed that everyone had a right to education, but this was difficult to put into practice because there were few schools or teachers. He also began building a road and railroad link between Guayaquil and Quito.

During the following years a conflict developed between Guayaquil on the coast, where the main interest was in trade and export, and Quito in the highlands, where the landowners, backed by the Church, remained powerful. In 1895 the coastal liberals under General Eloy Alfaro obtained the upper hand. Under Alfaro's presidency and that of his successor, General Leonidas Plaza, a number of reforms were carried out. Most significantly, they confiscated the Church's large estates, thus reducing its power and preventing it from interfering in the government of the country. Education was improved, and the railroad and road between Guayaquil and Quito were completed.

In the 1930s a remarkable political figure emerged who was acceptable to the people of both the coast and the highlands. He was José María Velasco Ibarra, and he subsequently became president of Ecuador five times between the years 1934 and 1972. His presidencies were interrupted by military coups, sudden and violent grabs of state power by small groups. However, from 1948 to 1952 there was a period of stability under the civilian government of Leonidas Plaza's son, Galo Plaza Lasso. In 1964 an Agrarian Reform Law was passed, which began to distribute land to peasants.

Large rivers, such as the Guayas in Ecuador, flow to the Pacific from the Andes. Ecuador's main port, Guayaquil, is at the mouth of this river.

It was not until 1979 that true democratic elections took place for the first time. Anyone over 18 years of age who was literate could vote, and Jaime Roldós Aguilera was elected president for a five-year term.

Peru and Bolivia

After independence some leaders felt Peru and Bolivia should be united. Peru invaded Bolivia in 1828, and for 13 years after that invasion, the two republics waged war. Neither side won, and in 1836 they agreed to form a Peru-Bolivia Confederation. Chile, their southern neighbor, opposed the confederation and brought it to an end at the battle of Yungay in 1839. For most of the next 50 years, the fortunes of Peru and Bolivia revolved around the exploitation of bird

The Chincha Islands off the coast of Peru are home to millions of seabirds. A century ago these islands brought great prosperity to coastal Peru when the bird droppings, or guano, were exported as a fertilizer.

droppings called guano and nitrate deposits on the coast, and the relationship of the two countries with Chile.

Guano was in great demand in Europe as a fertilizer and soon became Peru's major export. There were also guano deposits in one small part of the northern Atacama Desert owned by Bolivia. The region was very remote from the main Andean centers of Bolivia, and when the Chileans invaded the territory, the Bolivians could not defend it. The guano trade was so profitable that at one point Spain tried to regain control of Peru's Chincha Islands, but the greater threat came from Chile. Gradually, the guano deposits were used up, but by then the Chileans had discovered that the Atacama Desert was rich in nitrate deposits, which were also used as a fertilizer. In the Bolivian section they had found silver, too. When Chile took the main Bolivian nitrate deposits by force and began to threaten Peru, war was inevitable. The War of the Pacific lasted from 1879 to 1883 and was a total victory for Chile. Bolivia lost all its coastal territory, and Peru lost some of its richest nitrate deposits.

During most of this period, both countries were led by ambitious, corrupt, and ruthless caudillos. After the war political parties developed and a period of peace and civilian rule followed. Heavy debt forced Peru and Bolivia to seek foreign help. In return for trade concessions, British investors financed and expanded the railroads so that minerals could be transported from the highlands to the coast. Around the turn of the century, United States investors began to take over from the British. They backed public construction projects and became involved in major industries, such as shipping, minerals, oil, sugar, and textiles. However, this commercial progress only benefited a small group of people. Real power and wealth remained in the hands of a few farming and mining families, with the poor continuing to survive as best they could.

The Chaco War

In the 1930s Bolivia fought a devastating war with Paraguay over an area of land between the two countries called the Chaco. The Chaco was thought to contain oil, but for Bolivia it could have meant a route to the sea by way of the Plate River system. Thousands of Bolivia's Indians were sent into battle, and because they were ill-equipped and undernourished, they died. The plight of the Indians was there for all to see, and a new generation of politicians resolved that something must be done. In 1941 Victor Paz Estenssoro founded the Bolivian National Revolutionary Movement and was later elected president of the country four times.

Reform and revolution

In 1924 the Peruvian Víctor Raúl Haya de la Torre created a political party called APRA, which represented the interests of ordinary people in Peru and criticized the power of its North American businessmen. It drew support from the middle and working classes but was opposed by the majority of landowners and the military. Since World War II Peru has had military and civilian governments. They have dealt with some basic economic and social problems, but it was not until 1964, under President Fernando Belaúnde, that a limited reform was introduced, making tenant farmers owners of their land. Some Indians received land, but many large estates were left untouched. In 1968 Belaúnde was removed from office by a left-wing military coup, which divided up the estates and nationalized, or put into state ownership, several large foreign companies.

Over the border in Bolivia, there had been countless changes in government and some 170 coups since independence, but in 1952 a revolutionary government was elected under Victor Paz Estenssoro and the National Revolutionary Movement party. With the powerful political backing of the miners and ordinary people, his government introduced a

The Bolivian National Revolutionary Movement party led the way to major social reforms with a revolution on April 9, 1952. Each year when the party was in power the revolution was honored with lengthy parades.

41

Che Guevara in Bolivia
Che Guevara was Argentinian, a prominent Communist, and a guerrilla fighter who helped Fidel Castro gain power in Cuba in 1959. He was very influenced by the poverty he saw while traveling in Latin America as a student and resolved that the only solution was violent revolution. He fought alongside Castro and his brother, Raúl, in their successful campaign to overthrow the dictator Batista in Cuba. Guevara became a Cuban citizen and a member of Castro's Marxist government. He also wrote important books and manuals. He believed in taking revolution to all parts of the continent and in 1966 went to Bolivia to lead a guerrilla group. In 1967 he was captured and shot in the Andean foothills near Sucre.

program of radical land ownership. Everyone was given the right to vote, the tin mines were nationalized, and there was a genuine reform of the land-ownership system so that all the Indians received land. To support the reforms, however, the government needed financing. Although the United States gave considerable help, Paz Estenssoro was ousted by the military in 1964 when the economy got out of hand. All successive governments, though, have upheld the changes he made in 1952.

Government today
During the 1980s all three countries had stable, democratically elected governments. There were no coups, and the military did not attempt to take over. The greatest problem facing Ecuador, Peru,

and Bolivia as developing countries is an economic one. Ecuador discovered great quantities of oil in the 1970s, but oil prices slumped in the 1980s. And from 1984 to 1988, under President Léon Febres Cordero, the country suffered a severe recession.

In Bolivia Victor Paz Estenssoro was re-elected in 1984 and inherited a virtually bankrupt country with the highest inflation in the world. To buy a loaf of bread, people in La Paz had to carry shopping bags full of bundles of paper money. Estenssoro introduced successful anti-inflation measures, but in 1985 the world tin market collapsed and, with it, so did Bolivia's main export.

Peru has equally severe economic problems, but it also has a guerrilla problem. Neither the government of Fernando Belaúnde, re-elected in 1980, nor that of APRA leader Alan García Pérez, elected in 1985, has been able to halt the activities of a Marxist terrorist group called the "Shining Path." There are almost daily bomb attacks, often in the capital, Lima, and in 10 years, 15,000 people have been killed. The terrorists are thought to have influence over coca growers who supply dealers in the cocaine trade, some of whom, in Bolivia and Peru, are rich and powerful enough to threaten the stability of legal governments. Despite all the problems, it is encouraging that successful democratic elections have been held in recent years in all three republics.

4   People of the Andes

The native peoples of South America are called Indians because when Colombus arrived in the New World, he thought he had discovered the Indies. Different groups of Indians live in the highlands, on the coast, and in the forests. More than half the population of Bolivia is Quechua and Aymara Indians. When the Spaniards arrived, they intermarried with the Indians and created a new race called *mestizos*. The mestizos are now one of the the the largest groups in Ecuador and Peru. The African slaves who were brought to work in the mines and on the plantations also intermarried with the Indians, and left a smaller number of descendants. The remaining population is made up of the descendants of immigrants who arrived in the nineteenth century and small groups of whites and blacks who did not intermarry with the native peoples.

Andean Languages

After the Spanish Conquest of this part of South America, Spanish became the official language although many of the people of the Sierra, or highlands, have retained their original Quechua or Aymara to this day. In the 1970s Peru's military government decreed that Quechua should be taught as a national second language. This was a political move to give the Indian community more status. Pockets of other native languages have survived in remote parts of all three republics, particularly in the forested Amazonian region.

Sierra Indians

Quechua Indians live in the highlands of Ecuador, Peru, and southern Bolivia while most of the Aymara Indians live close to Lake Titicaca in southern Peru and northern Bolivia. The Aymara believe their god of creation, Viracocha, rose from the waters of the lake, and the Quechua creation legend tells of white, bearded men who came to their land, taught the people to sow crops, and then sailed away to the west.

In many ways the life-style and daily routine of the Quechua and Aymara are very similar, but the way they dress is different. Aymara women mostly wear huge colorful skirts, or *polleras*, with several petticoats at one time. These skirts are usually made from heavy cotton or wool, but for special occasions, they can be of velvet, silk, or

A Quechua Indian from Chivay in Peru, in traditional dress, carries her baby in her colorful aguayo *shawl.*

satin. A curious feature of Aymara dress is the way women wear bowler hats, which they are said to have adopted from the British workmen who arrived late in the nineteenth century to build the railroads. Quechua women wear just one long skirt, less colorful than the Aymara, but each village has its own style of hat. Women from both groups wear shawls, or *aguayos*, and use them to carry their babies or market produce on their backs. The most distinctive features of the men's dress are their striped ponchos, sandals made from the rubber of old tires, and knitted hats with earflaps, called *chullos*. Today many more Indian men are wearing western-style trousers and jackets.

Most Sierra Indians are subsistence farmers. They have a small plot of land and grow enough crops for themselves, taking any surplus to local markets to sell. Their homes are in scattered communities, often far from towns. They provide most of what they need for themselves, but their life is not easy. Their bodies have adapted to living at very high altitudes, but they still face harsh conditions. The climate is usually very hot or very cold, and the soil is poor. Whole families live together in small adobe, or mud-brick, homes. Their day starts at dawn and finishes at sunset. The women look after the cooking and weave clothes for the family while the men work on the land. Children, if not at school, look after llamas and tend sheep in the open, dry pastures.

Otavalo Indians
The Otavalo Indians, who live in the Sierra north of Quito in Ecuador, are exceptional because they

are commercially successful. They have exploited their traditional weaving skills, and they sell their goods throughout the Andes. Tourists flock to the Otavalo Saturday market, where cotton and woolen ponchos, sweaters, shawls, belts, hats, and other goods are on sale. Originally, the Otavalos wove everything by hand on old-fashioned upright looms. For some years now, though, they have had machines, and this has allowed them to expand their business.

The color of the Otavalos' clothes is predominantly blue. Men wear knee-length, dark blue ponchos over white breeches, and wide-brimmed straw hats or hats made of soft felt. They tie their black hair into a single braid that reaches halfway down their backs. Women cover their hair with blue headscarves, carry their babies in midnight-blue and white aguayos, and wear long, navy-blue skirts. Around their necks they wear many rows of gold-colored beads.

Another group of Indians in the Ecuadorian Sierra who are successful weavers are the Salasaca. They sell stylishly patterned textiles to tourists in the local markets.

The Uru-Chipaya

The Uru-Chipaya were widespread in the Andes at the time of the Spanish Conquest. They spoke a common language, but after the Conquest the Urus and Chipayas were forced into remote parts of the mountains and the two groups became separated. Today, a few hundred Chipaya survive in remote salt marshes in the west of Bolivia, but the last Uru died in the 1950s. Other Indian tribes disliked the Chipaya, and now, isolated, they

Women of the isolated Chipaya tribe in western Bolivia wear homespun garments made from sheep and llama wool. Their hairstyle of many braids has remained unchanged for hundreds of years.

lead a very primitive existence. Their adobe mud homes are round with domed, thatched roofs, no windows, and one door, which faces away from the prevailing wind. The door is of cactus wood because there are no trees in the area.

The Chipaya call themselves the "people of the tombs." Tombs, or *chullpas*, like small mud houses are found in the hills near their villages. In them mummies have been found dressed in much the same clothes and with similar hairstyles to the ones the Chipaya use today. It is the custom for the women to wear their hair in many tiny braids, and all their clothing is woven from the wool of llamas and sheep in natural beige and brown colors. The men wear tunics over baggy trousers, and the women wear blouses of rough cloth, shawls, and long black skirts.

The Chipaya were a hunting tribe. Today, they tend a few llamas or sheep, but they still hunt birds using a *bolas*. This is a Y-shaped cord weighted with stones, and with it they bring down ducks, geese, and sometimes flamingos as they fly over the salt marshes.

The last of the Urus lived on floating islands of totora reed in Lake Titicaca. Today, these are inhabited by Aymara Indians. Traditionally, the people of the islands fish then trade their catch in local markets. Many tourists visit the islands, and some changes are taking place. Most of the Indians' homes are made of totora reed, but a school has been built of corrugated iron, and many of the islanders now have transistor radios and other modern goods.

Forest and coastal Indians

Nobody can be sure how many tribes of Indians live in the Amazon forests. Some have been known about since missionaries first penetrated the lowlands soon after the Spanish Conquest. Other tribes are still being discovered. The missionaries continue to work in the forests, building small schools and introducing the Indians to Western ways, but it is very difficult for the forest people to find a place for themselves in the rest of society. If they do, they find themselves living in very poor conditions, on the outskirts of towns, without jobs or money. Some, like the Shipibo of Peru, use forest dyes like the red *achiote* and black *genipa* to make prettily decorated ceramics and cloths, which they sell to tourists.

The Indians who remain in the forest have a very primitive way of life. They build their houses of palm thatch and use palm wood for bows and arrows. The women weave cotton from the jungle, though the Yuracares of Bolivia use bark cloth for clothing. Forest Indians live on the wildlife of the jungle, hunting monkeys, rodents, and wild pigs. Others, like the Jivaros of Ecuador, once a headhunting tribe, grow a starchy root called manioc, another called *yuca*, and plantains. All forest Indians live under the constant threat of having their homeland destroyed. With the discovery of oil in the eastern lowlands of all three countries, new roads are being built and settlers are moving in from the highlands. All the Indians can do is fight back with their bows and arrows or move deeper into the forest.

Very few Amazon tribes have successfully retained their identity as more of the forest is settled by outsiders. A few groups like the Nahua of Peru have held out by hiding in remote places. The first recent contact with travelers was not until 1985.

The few Indians of the coast make their living fishing, farming, or working for local traders. The

Cayapa of Ecuador fish from carved dugout canoes on the Guayas River, and they raise cattle. The only other indigenous group, the Colorados, live near the town of Santo Domingo, where they farm. The Colorados or "Red Ones" are so-called because of the red dye, achiote, which they use to color their hair and paint their bodies. They wear a mixture of traditional and modern dress, and it is not unusual to see Colorado women in their knee-length, wraparound striped skirts and high rubber boots.

Mestizos

As more mixed marriages took place between Europeans and Indians and then mestizos and Indians, their mestizo descendants have become very numerous in the Andean countries. Mestizos have held the highest offices in their lands, from president downward. Many have professional positions as lawyers, doctors, and teachers while others manage big businesses. Less well-off mestizos may be miners, taxi drivers, domestic servants, or manual laborers. The work that mestizos get depends on how much education they receive, and most prefer to live in the towns where the schools and medical facilities are better. Most mestizos adopt a Western style of dress and follow the fashion trends of Europe and the United States closely. Jeans and tennis shoes are found as much in jungle towns as they are in capital cities.

Mestizos in Bolivia are sometimes known as *cholos*. In La Paz the women, or *cholas*, trade in the markets and on the city streets, selling anything from internationally manufactured cosmetics to

A mestizo and a Colorado Indian jog together. Colorado Indians of eastern Ecuador take their name from the red dye with which they color their hair and paint their bodies. Settlers have moved into their land, but they have retained their identity and largely rejected the ways of newcomers.

local produce. They dress traditionally in bowler hats and pollera skirts. Cholas are said to be among the wealthiest people in the capital.

The number of descendants of African slaves and Indians is relatively small, and they live mainly in the coastal areas. There, they farm, fish, and trade.

Minorities

The remainder of the population is made up of small groups such as the descendants of black slaves from Africa. There are still communities, such as that of the blacks of the Chota valley in Ecuador, who have retained their African identity and have not intermarried with the local population. The African women wear ankle-length, African-style dresses, and their houses are made of thatch in an African style. In the nineteenth century Chinese people were brought to Peru to work on the railroads under the British, and their stores and restaurants are evidence of their presence in every major town in the country. There is a Chinese community near Guayaquil, and recently other Chinese from Hong Kong have arrived in Bolivia. Guayaquil also has a number of Lebanese merchants. In the southeast of Bolivia, near the town of Santa Cruz, there is a colony of Japanese settlers. Germans sought refuge in the three republics both before and after World War II, and in La Paz many run small delis.

There is also a small number of descendants of the original Spanish settlers who have not intermarried with the local people. This small minority, particularly in Ecuador and Peru, forms the elite of local society.

When African slaves were brought to Ecuador some 300 years ago, some escaped to the Andes. Some of their descendants, such as this community in the Chota valley 4,003 feet (1,220 meters) above sea level, have remained isolated and have kept much of their African identity.

5   Living and Working

In Bolivia most people live and work in the highlands, where the main towns and mining centers have developed. In Ecuador and Peru the working population is divided almost equally between the coast and the Sierra.

Towns and cities
Outside La Paz, the most important city in Bolivia is Cochabamba, situated at a lower altitude in a fertile agricultural region. Sucre, a quiet, colonial town not far from Cochabamba, was the capital of Bolivia until the late nineteenth century. Life in these two towns is considerably more pleasant than in Oruro, center of the tin-mining industry, and Potosí, where conditions have deteriorated because tin and silver no longer bring such high prices. The fastest-growing town in Bolivia is Santa Cruz in the Oriente. Thirty years ago Santa Cruz was a town of mud streets, which could only be negotiated by horses or four-wheel drive jeep taxis, but discoveries of oil and gas have led to rapid development and a 400 percent increase in population.

In Ecuador the port of Guayaquil has the largest population although Quito, in the highlands, is the capital. The old city of Cuenca, founded by the Spaniards in 1557 in the southern highlands, is Ecuador's third largest city. Other towns on the coast are Esmeraldas, Ecuador's fifth largest city, and Manta, which is its main commercial center west of Guayaquil and has steep streets and a fine wooden church. Puyo is

In Lima, Peru, the Plaza San Martin, named after the independence hero General José de San Martin, was once the thriving heart of the city. Many businesses have now moved to modern suburbs.

the only town of any size in the Oriente. As more settlers move in, modern concrete buildings are replacing the wooden ones.

Peru has many urban centers on the coast and in the Sierra, but the city of Lima, with its port, Callao, is by far the largest. Half the country's town dwellers live there. Other important industrial towns on the coast include Chimbote, the country's largest fishing port. Trujillo, in a fertile oasis on the northern coast, challenges Arequipa, in the southern highlands, for the position of being Peru's second largest city. Arequipa, at 7,808 feet (2,380 meters), lies at the foot of the majestic, snowcapped volcano, El Misti. Cuzco, the old Incan capital, is still an important city and is visited by many tourists every year. In the northeast Peru's Amazon port, Iquitos, can still be reached only by air or river.

Living conditions and migration

Most towns in Ecuador, Peru, and Bolivia are a mixture of Spanish colonial buildings and modern highrise office buildings. Depending on their status and wealth, people working in the towns may live in tree-lined, residential suburbs, apartment buildings, or, occasionally, new middle-class housing developments. The houses are mostly built of brick or reinforced concrete because of the threat of earthquakes. By contrast, homes in the rural highlands are made of adobe or stone, and homes on the coast are made of reed or cane or wattle and daub.

In recent years many people have moved from

Shantytowns, like this one in the desert outside Lima, have developed as more people move from rural areas into the cities. Here people line up to collect water.

rural areas into the towns. For the poorer, rural people, the towns have a great attraction. They offer schools, hospitals, running water, sanitation, lighting, and other modern amenities. Sadly, though, the urban centers are unable to cope with this large influx of people, who find themselves living in shantytowns, without any amenities, on the outskirts. Outside Lima, in the desert, there are sprawling suburbs of people whose homes are shacks made of cardboard, cane, and mud. The authorities have tried to set up building programs of new towns with better facilities, but they cannot keep pace with the number of people who arrive each day.

Several governments have also introduced colonization projects, encouraging people to move from the Sierra to the Oriente, but these plans have not met with much success either. People from the highlands find it difficult to adapt to the Oriente's hot, wet climate. Farming techniques and produce are different there, and the people are vulnerable to tropical diseases.

Family life
The poorer families in the countryside or those who have migrated to the towns are usually large. This is necessary because everyone has to work to help the family survive. Grandparents are cared for within the family, but they, in turn, look after the younger members of the family or help with household chores. Young children take on responsibility at an early age. Like her mother, a five- or six-year-old girl will carry a younger sister or brother in an aguayo on her back while helping to sell goods in the market. Boys are sent into the

Many children in these Andean countries leave school to help earn money for their families. Selling candy and gum is easy but unrewarding.

towns to do odd jobs, sell trinkets, or clean cars. In Quito, there are so many young shoeshine boys that a charity set up a school to give them at least a few lessons and something to eat.

Women's Role
In the towns many more women go out to work. With the older children at school and grandparents looking after the young, the mother is able to earn money by trading in the markets, selling bread or other foods on the street, or working as a domestic servant in one of the wealthier households. It has always been the custom for men to be given greater freedom than women, but today, women also work in offices, banks, and shops. Others are employed by the government, and a few have qualified in top professions. In Bolivia the first chola senator has been elected, and the country has had one woman president, Lydia Gueller Tejada.

Going to school

Schools in Ecuador, Peru, and Bolivia are run both by the state and the Catholic Church. There are also a few private schools that charge tuition. Although the law in all three republics says that all children from the age of six or seven to 14 should attend school, it is not possible to enforce this law. In the towns the majority of children do go to school, but because there are often not enough classrooms, two sessions of lessons are taught each day. The young children go in the morning, and the older students go in the afternoon. The curriculum covers mathematics, science, history, geography, and languages.

Rural children are not so fortunate. Sierra Indian families often do not allow their children to attend, particularly young girls who have to look after the animals. If the children are allowed

Since the revolution of 1952, the Bolivian government has made great efforts to take education to even the remotest areas. These children are at school in a mountain village more than 62 miles (100 kilometers) from the nearest town.

to go, they might have to walk many miles each day to reach their school. There are fewer schools in rural areas, and they are poorly equipped. The Indian children have the added problem of having to learn Spanish, which is the language they are taught in, although their native language is Quechua or Aymara. Even so, an increasing number of children are learning to read and write. Literacy programs, both for adults and children, have been helped considerably by lessons that are broadcast on the radio. Even the remotest communities usually have access to a radio.

A large proportion of students go on to a high-school, technical, or college education. Most of the major cities have a university or technical college. The University of San Marcos in Lima and the University of Chuquisaca in Sucre date from the early sixteenth century and are two of the oldest in the Americas. It is unfortunate for these developing countries that too many of their well-educated, trained professionals leave to work in the United States and Europe, where facilities are better and salaries are higher.

Food and markets

Potatoes were first grown in the Andes, and the Indians have a traditional way of preserving them. The potatoes are laid out in the hot sun, and the women tread them to squeeze out the water. They leave the shriveled potatoes spread out in the fields to freeze at night, and the freeze-dried *chuño*, as it is called, can be kept in good condition for months.

The most common family meal in the Sierra is a form of stew made of meat, vegetables, and *quinoa*, a nutritious native cereal. Chickens are widely available, and Indians also eat guinea pigs, which they rear in their homes. The coastal people eat a variety of local fish, often with rice, and a stew, or *sancocho*, made with meat, bananas, and *yuca*. A specialty in Peru is *anticuchos*. These are pieces of meat arranged on a skewer, rather like kebabs, which are cooked on stoves on street corners and eaten as a snack. Other local Andean favorites are *empañadas*, small pastries filled with meat or cheese, and *humitas*, ears of sweet corn cooked in their husks. Andean people like their food hot and spicy.

The Indians make many drinks from natural starchy foods. In the Andes corn is used for *chicha*. After mixing the ground corn with boiled

61

The Otavalo Indian Saturday market has local produce and woven goods for sale. Many tourists visit the market to buy from the fine selection of ponchos, sweaters, and other goods made by the Otavalo Indians.

water, the mixture is allowed to ferment, producing a thick, mildly alcoholic drink. Less traditional, Coca Cola has been for sale almost everywhere in the Andes for many years, and in Peru one company has produced a competitor, Inca Cola. Now the hamburger and hot dog have arrived. Trendy new snackbars have opened in the main towns, and young teenagers are acquiring a taste for the new fast food.

For the growing middle class in the towns, there are supermarkets and grocery stores, but often traditional markets offer a greater variety of meat, fruit, and vegetables. In La Paz, because there is a black market of goods that are imported illegally, almost anything can be bought, at a price, from Scottish smoked fish to French cheese. Rural markets are social gathering places. At least once a week people get together to trade their animals, crops, and weavings.

Herbal and modern medicine

For many families in the Andean republics, the staple foods are potatoes, rice, and bread. Other foods like meat and milk are expensive or hard to get. Fruit, which is plentiful in the lowlands, is often overripe by the time it reaches the highlands. This limited diet results in many of the poorer people suffering from malnutrition. Some government and international agencies have financed food programs.

These same agencies, which include the United Nations and the World Health Organization, have also worked with local ministries of health to reduce or stamp out diseases like yellow fever, cholera, malaria, and smallpox. Other diseases, like typhoid and hepatitis, are carried in polluted water, and even now, in many towns, it is unsafe to drink the water.

Although there are hospitals and medical units in most towns, there are few in rural areas. Some mobile units serve outlying villages, but there are not enough trained doctors or nurses prepared to work far from the urban centers. Equipment is often outdated and medicine expensive. Some workers benefit from government-run social security and health plans, but many of the Sierra Indians reject modern medicine, preferring their own herbal cures. To stave off hunger, and as a medicine, Sierra Indians chew the coca leaf. They have done this for many centuries, and no man will set off for a day's work without his leaves.

6   Religion and Recreation

In Incan times the festival of Inti Raimi marked the midwinter day, which is in June in the Andes. The same festival is still remembered by the Indians and celebrated annually in the fortress of Sacsayhuaman, Cuzco.

Since the time of the Incas, the Andean people, particularly in rural areas, have enjoyed fiestas as a time to relax. The Incas had a calendar of festivals, which were mostly associated with working on the land. Each month in the agricultural year was significant. For example, in the first month they honored the Storm God because they needed rain to make the seeds grow. In June, after harvest, came the most important festival in honor of Inti Raimi, the Sun God. In August they held the festival of Pachamama, Mother Earth, because it was the

month of plowing. Many Andean people still honor the gods and spirits they believe exist in the natural world by sacrificing llamas or sheep and by sprinkling alcohol on the earth.

Public Holidays
During the Spanish Conquest and subsequent battles for independence, public holidays were created to celebrate the foundations of cities, the anniversaries of battles, and to honor heroes like Simón Bolívar. On these occasions civic and military authorities officiate at parades that last all day. The parades are sometimes very colorful, with many marchers in uniform and bands playing regimental music. There are so many public holidays that governments have tried to reduce their numbers.

The Catholic Church

When the Spaniards arrived in South America, they tried to crush the native people's belief in gods and spirits. They destroyed idols and shrines and, instead, built magnificent churches and convents. The Indians clung to their beliefs, however, so the Spanish priests adopted a policy of associating Catholic ritual with Indian tradition. In the center of Cuzco, the Incas had their holiest shrine, the Temple of the Sun. Rather than destroy it completely, the Spaniards built their own church of Santo Domingo on top of its remains. Festivals were set to coincide so that Indians and Spaniards could celebrate at the same time. Throughout the colonial period the Catholic Church was powerful, and missionaries continued to work in all parts of the Andes, converting the people. Today, the majority of the population is nominally Catholic although the Indian peoples still believe in Pachamama and other gods.

Most churches in Ecuador, Peru, and Bolivia remain open all day long. They are never empty. People attend mass from early in the morning, and for many of the poor, the church is a sanctuary where they can rest and pray and light candles to a favorite saint. Great importance is placed on family occasions that take place in the church, such as baptisms, weddings, and funerals. For their first communion girls from even the poorest families wear pretty white dresses decorated with lace or satin. The religious celebrations of Christmas, Holy Week, and Easter also have a special place in Andean life.

Weddings are a great opportunity for celebration in any Andean community. The couple meet at the church for a simple service, and afterward the entire village joins the party.

Fiestas

Fiesta time in the Andes is always colorful, noisy, and great fun. Two of the best known fiestas have religious associations. One is the *Diablada,* or Devil Dance, which takes place before Lent in Oruro, in Bolivia. The theme of the dance is the contest between good and evil. For many months beforehand, skilled workers prepare the elaborate costumes. The dancers wear heavy, grotesque masks, decorated with plaster snakes or toads. They have huge bulging, painted eyes and large triangular, glass teeth. The carnival lasts for several days, with dancers leaping and pirouetting through the streets to the sound of trumpets and drums.

The Corpus Christi celebrations in Cuzco in Peru are a more somber affair. Statues of saints from churches in and around Cuzco are paraded through the city on platforms, led by priests and surrounded by crowds of people chanting and carrying candles. The pageant of Inti Raimi is held at the same time. It takes place in the Incan temple-fortress of Sacsayhuaman on a hill just outside Cuzco and is a big tourist attraction. Hundreds of dancers, dressed in Incan-style tunics, and an emperor carried in on a litter celebrate the Festival of the Sun.

The Alacitas Fair is a folkloric fiesta, held by the Aymara Indians in the region of La Paz in Bolivia. It is in honor of Ekeko, symbolized by a tiny silver figure laden with miniature household and personal objects. Ekeko brings good luck, and at the fair people buy miniature replicas of goods they would like to acquire, like a television set or a car or bundles of money.

67

The elaborately costumed group, La Morenada, is one of the major dance groups of the Oruro Carnival.

Other fiestas are rather more barbaric. A few communities have annual battles to gain land and crops from each other. They fight on horseback, using slingshots and stones, and the battle is only considered won once one side has killed an opponent!

Some of the finest mountain ranges in the Andes are in Bolivia, and Mount Chacaltaya at 17,060 feet (5,200 meters) claims the world's highest ski slope.

Sports and games

It is possible to enjoy almost any sport in the three republics. In the mountains people walk, climb, and ski. Mount Chacaltaya, near La Paz, has the highest ski slope in the world. The Pacific waves off the Peru coast are excellent for surfing, but people also sail, waterski, and fish. In the larger towns there are golf, tennis, and swimming clubs and facilities for table tennis, pool, and cycling.

Unfortunately, only a few people can afford to enjoy many of these sports. Soccer, basketball, and volleyball, though, are sports that everybody can take part in. Any opportunity is taken to kick a ball around in the street or on a spare piece of land. Soccer is the most popular game, and there are national and local teams. Any match, and

People of all the Andean countries enjoy sports and quickly turn a street or field into a place for a game. These people are in Sepahua, a Peruvian Amazon village.

particularly the World Cup, arouses great excitement. Supporters fill the stadiums, crowd around televisions, and, in remote regions, listen to their radios. When their team wins, supporters drive around the streets with their car horns blaring, wave flags, and have parties that go on long into the night.

Andean families also enjoy the traditional bullfights originally introduced by the Spaniards. Lima has the oldest bullring in the Americas, and there are two bullfight seasons each year. Cockfights are still held in some small villages. A favorite game that needs some skill and a good eye is *sapo*. To gain a high score, solid bronze disks have to be tossed into the open mouth of a bronze frog on a board containing many other holes.

7   Arts, Crafts, and Music

Objects found in graves on the Peruvian coast show that the people of the ancient civilizations, although they used only simple tools, were skilled goldsmiths, weavers, and potters. Gold was shaped and fashioned in a variety of ways and used for practical as well as decorative purposes. Many examples of masks, breastplates, drinking cups, and pieces of jewelry have been found. The weavings of the Paracas culture were some of the finest ever made. The potters of Nasca and Moche produced ceramics of many colors, shapes, and designs. One unusual design was the stirrup pot, which had two spouts joined by a ceramic bridge. The pots were decorated with designs of animals, birds, heads of warriors, and scenes from everyday life.

The Incas were excellent stonemasons. Walls of their buildings remain today. They were made of huge blocks of stone, carved and fitted together so tightly that a knife blade will not pass between them. The stone was quarried in the mountains, and the men transported it. With some blocks weighing over 100 tons, this was an amazing feat, especially because the Incas had no knowledge of the wheel. Some of the largest blocks were used to build Sacsayhuaman.

Colonial art

Spanish missionaries recognized the artistic talents of the native people and founded a few schools where their skills could be encouraged. The Franciscan priest, Pedro Gosseal, established

71

Spanish craftsmen taught the Andean Indians the technique for gilding and painting, so their churches became remarkable places of worship. The Church of La Compañia in Quito is perhaps the most lavishly decorated.

one of these schools in Quito in about 1550. The Indians learned about European painting and sculpture and how to carve in wood. Most of what they made was for religious use. They worked on carved pulpits and statues for churches and missions and paintings depicting religious images. European influence is evident in the work of two of the leading seventeenth-century Andean painters, the Indian, Diego Quispe Tito of Cuzco, and Melchor Pérez de Holguín from Bolivia. By the eighteenth century some mestizo and Indian artists, known as the Cuzco School, were portraying more native themes. The greatest Indian sculptor was Manuel Chili, known as *Caspicara*, from Quito.

Some of the best examples of colonial architecture are the churches and cathedrals. Many copied the high-vaulted gothic style of Europe. Others have lavishly carved facades with statues of Christ or the saints. Some of the interiors are breathtakingly beautiful, with magnificent altars of gold and silver leaf and ceilings covered with glazed tiles.

Twentieth Century
This century artists have turned to their own traditions and culture for inspiration. They have been influenced by political and revolutionary change and the plight of the Andean Indians. Ecuador's foremost painter, Osvaldo Guayasamín, whose father was an Indian, was the eldest of 10 children. As a young boy he sold his sketches on the streets of Quito, but only a few years later he was exhibiting internationally. The Peruvian artist José Sabogal contrasts the plight of the Indians today with the cultural achievements of their Incan ancestors. In Bolivia Guzmán de Rojas and María Luisa Pacheco have been among the leading artists who use native subjects. The two best-known sculptors are Joaquín Roca Rey from Peru and Marina Núñez del Prado from Bolivia.

Writers and poets

The early Incas had no writing. The first writers Ecuador, Peru, and Bolivia produced were the Spanish chroniclers, mostly soldiers and priests, who left descriptions of what life was like under the Inca empire and in the early days of the new colonies. The first great mestizo writer was Garcilaso de la Vega, who wrote the historical *Royal Commentaries of the Inca* in 1609.

Toward the end of the colonial period when people became aware of the struggle for freedom from oppression going on in Europe, their literature began to challenge Spanish influence and authority. Writers and poets were among the first to call for independence. The Ecuadorian José Joaquín Olmedo wrote poems about the struggle for independence and the civil war that followed in Ecuador. After independence from Spain had been won, the writers, like the artists, were concerned with political and social wrongs and wrote passionately about the sufferings of the Indians. Two of the most important writers at the start of this century were the Peruvians Clorinda Matto de Turner and Manuel González Prada. In the twentieth century many novels examine what has happened to the Indians, although not always sympathetically. In his *Race of Bronze,* the Bolivian writer Alcides Arguedas criticizes Indians for being weak, while his contemporaries, Franz Tamayo and Ricardo Jaimes Freyre, write of the Indians' strength.

José Carlos Mariátegui was an intellectual who founded the Peruvian Communist party in 1928. He also produced an influential magazine, *Amauta,* to which many radical left-wing writers contributed political essays. One of his followers, and one of Peru's most successful writers, is Ciro Alegria, whose novels include *The Golden Serpent* and *Broad and Alien is the World*. Mario Vargas Llosa is the best-known writer from the region today. Like many of his predecessors, Vargas Llosa is deeply concerned for the future of his country. He is actively involved in politics, and in 1990 he ran in, but lost, the presidential election in Peru. His novels include *Conversation in the Cathedral* and *War at the End of the World*.

Music and dance

The music of the three republics derives from the Spanish, Andean, and African origins of the people. The Spaniards introduced the first string instruments, such as the guitar. The Andean people have adapted the shape of the Spanish guitar to make a native instrument called a *charango*. The average charango is about 12 inches (30.5 centimeters) long with five pairs of strings and a back made of an armadillo shell. The Spaniards also brought with them the violin and the harp, and the Andean people have adapted the European harp so they can carry it during fiestas and processions.

In recent years groups have been invited to play Andean music in theaters in Europe and the United States. They have helped to make the haunting sound of the panpipes of the Andes more familiar. Clay panpipes more than a thousand years old have been dug up in Nasca on the coast of Peru. Today's pipes are made from reed and bamboo, and the most common kind is the *sicu* with a double row of mouthpieces.

These traditional reed panpipes, or zampoñas, *are still used by Andean Indians in the way they were by their ancestors more than 1,000 years ago.*

Other wind instruments include the *quena, tarka,* and *pinquillo,* all forms of the flute. In addition to strings, pipes, and flutes, a typical local band playing at fiesta time has a variety of drums, and sometimes trumpets. In remoter parts of the republics, people make unusual instruments out of whatever materials are available. These include the *pututu,* made from cow horn, and the *concha,* which is a seashell. Both of these are wind instruments, but the people like to use gourds filled with seeds as percussion instruments, too.

One popular Andean dance is the *cueca,* in which the dancers wave a handkerchief. This is derived from a favorite Spanish colonial dance. Another dance popular since the time of the

Spanish Conquest is the *wayno,* and the music for it is played endlessly in Peruvian villages. Elements of the distinctive African rhythm are still heard on the coast, but it is the native music of the Andes that is most typical of the region.

Weaving and basketry

Weaving has been part of the cultural traditions of the Andean and coastal peoples for thousands of years. The burial cloths found in the Paracas graves are evidence of this. They are colorful, showing supernatural, human, and animal figures on dark backgrounds and were dyed with a large variety of natural pigments. They also show that ancient weavers knew most of the techniques known and employed today. In graves of other cultures, cloths decorated with feathers and metalwork have been discovered.

Weaving is a traditional craft of the Andean Indian women. This Aymara Indian woman is weaving an aguaya shawl on a loom outside her hut.

The Chancay culture produced small embroidered, cloth dolls.

The basic materials used by weavers then and now are cotton grown in the valleys and wool from llamas and alpacas. In most Indian communities women do the spinning and weaving. For spinning yarn the Indian women prefer a drop spindle, which they can use while tending their animals or walking to market. The spinning wheel introduced by the Spaniards is much less versatile. For weaving, two types of looms are popular. The back-strap loom has the advantage of being easy to carry. The weaver keeps one strap behind her back and ties the other end to a tree or post. This loom is useful for weaving small items like belts and headbands. Larger pieces of cloth, for skirts and ponchos, are woven on horizontal looms, which are staked into the ground outside the family hut. In the sixteenth century Europeans introduced the treadle loom. On this type of loom, today's weavers produce rugs, wall-hangings, and textiles for the tourist and commercial market.

The Indians, particularly those of Ecuador, also make baskets and other household items. Basketry is a traditional craft among them, and the articles they produce also find a ready market in tourist shops.

8   Keeping in Touch

Good overland transportation connections are essential for the development and unity of any country. In the Andean republics this is particularly difficult to achieve. The steep slopes of the Andes are a formidable barrier between the coast and the Amazon lowlands.

When the Spanish soldiers first arrived, they found the Incas had an excellent system of roads. Two main highways connected the empire from north to south, and there were branching roads to the coast and eastern Andean slopes. The roads were mostly long and straight and, in the towns, often paved or cobbled. Rivers and gorges were crossed by suspension bridges made of fiber ropes, and storehouses were built alongside the roads so that supplies were available whenever the emperor or his nobles traveled.

The Incas had no form of wheeled transportation, and the emperor was carried in a litter on the shoulders of his men. Messages and some goods were relayed by a system of runners called *chasquis*, each of whom covered a distance of about a mile before passing the message or item to the next runner. In this way, fish were carried from the coast to the emperor's table in Cuzco in just two days.

Many of the Incan roads still exist today, but the developing economy, particularly the transportation of minerals, demanded a more sophisticated level of communication. The introduction of railroads in the nineteenth century and of air transportation in the twentieth, together with better roads, have all contributed greatly to this higher communication level. All are difficult and expensive to maintain, however, particularly in view of the distances, heights, and unpredictable weather conditions.

By road
Some roads in the region, on the desert coast and in the Altiplano in Bolivia, are long, flat, straight as far as the eye can see, and usually paved. Roads in the mountains, though, present great technical problems, and those connecting the highlands to the Amazon lowlands are some of the most spectacular in South America. Often the width of just one vehicle, the roads zigzag around the mountain curves, which have sheer rock faces and terrifying precipices sometimes 2,000 feet (610 meters) deep. The curves are so tortuous that drivers cannot see vehicles coming in the opposite direction, and accidents are frequent. Rains wash away the sides of these roads, and landslides can stop traffic for many days.

High in the mountains, roads are usually of hardened dirt. They run through open countryside, across riverbeds, and between mountain passes, some of 16,000 feet (4,877 meters). The rainy season turns many of these roads into extended mud tracks that only large, powerful vehicles can negotiate. Few roads have penetrated far into the Amazon lowlands. In the 1960s President Belaúnde of Peru dreamed of building a *Carretera Marginal* to connect the Andean countries along the edge of these lowlands. Some parts of the road were constructed, but the cost of forging a route

Precipitous roads have been cut along the mountainsides of the eastern Andes of Bolivia, taking traffic from the highlands to the lowland Amazon forests.

through the impenetrable forests and swamps was too much, and the project was abandoned.

Every form of public transportation is used on the roads in Ecuador, Peru, and Bolivia. Long-distance buses are good although trips can take many hours. Many poorer people travel in the back of open trucks with their bundles and

81

In some Amazon towns motorbikes are the usual form of transportation and are often used as taxis, like these in Guayaramerín, Bolivia.

animals. In the jungle towns, motorbikes are very popular because they can be ridden anywhere in any weather.

By rail

The great age of railroad building in the Andes was in the late nineteenth and early twentieth centuries. One of the most remarkable achievements was the construction of the Central Railway in Peru, which runs from Callao, on the coast, through Lima to Huancayo in the central Andes. It is a relatively short journey of 107 miles (172 kilometers), but in that distance the railroad climbs from sea level to 15,689 feet (4,782 meters). A branch line to the mining town of Oroya is the

This vintage steam locomotive, built in Britain in 1947, still pulls trains along the line between Huancayo and Huancavelica in the Peruvian Andes.

highest railroad in the world. The railroad was begun in 1870 under the direction of a brilliant United States businessman, Henry Meiggs. Thousands of workers died during its construction, but the link was essential to carry minerals from mountains to coast. The Guayaquil to Quito railroad was almost as difficult to build. In one area, it climbs to 10,623 feet (3,238 meters) in 50 miles (80 kilometers).

Steam trains still operate in parts of the Andes, but gradually electric-powered trains are taking over. Maintaining a good railroad system is particularly important for Bolivia's export trade because it provides the country's main connection with coastal ports in Chile.

Railway King
Henry Meiggs was born in Catskill, New York, in 1811. He was a successful merchant before he was 20 and by 32 was manager of one of the United States' most powerful lumber firms. Four years later he lost most of his money when a bank collapsed, so he decided to go to California, where he made another fortune. He twice became mayor of the city of San Francisco and gave away money to many charitable organizations. In 1850 a fire destroyed much of the city, and Henry Meiggs lost his second fortune. He used illegal means to settle his huge debts. Eventually, he had to flee in a small steamship. He arrived in Chile a fugitive and virtually penniless. Within a few years, though, using his business skills and charm, he had built his first successful railroad. His reputation spread beyond Chile, and in 1868 he was invited to Peru. There he became involved in the construction of several railroads, including the Central Railway.

By air

Air transportation developed rapidly after World War I. Aircraft could go farther faster, so they had a great advantage over rail and road communication. Foreign investors helped set up the first airline companies, but today each country runs its own national airline. The three airlines are *Ecuatoriana, AeroPeru,* and *Lloyd Aereo Boliviano.* There are also several private companies. Their planes fly to many destinations in South America and connect with flights to the rest of the world. Major international airlines also fly into Ecuador, Peru, and Bolivia.

Weather conditions in the Andes can make flying very hazardous. Quito, set in a deep canyon surrounded by mountains, has poor visibility in heavy clouds. The runways of La Paz's airport are unusually long because, at that altitude, the thin air makes it especially hard for planes to brake and accelerate. On one short, notorious route in Bolivia, pilots have to use a stopwatch to time their turns as they negotiate their way through cloud-covered mountain peaks. Small, light aircraft and air taxis are increasingly popular in the Oriente, where they can land and take off using a hastily prepared patch of jungle terrain or a clearing in the forest. These planes have managed to contact some of the most isolated communities, and even primitive forest Indians are now accustomed to seeing them.

By water
For centuries people of the Oriente have relied on the rivers as their only form of communication.

The many Amazon tributaries are similar to a network of roads, and river boats transport a large variety of goods.

Today passengers and cargoes are carried in dugout canoes, small boats with outboard motors, and a kind of flat-bottomed barge with two or three decks. The craft have to be shallow because, particularly in the dry season, there are many hazards like sandbanks and fallen, submerged trees. Rapids in the tributaries of the Upper Amazon are also a real danger, even to the most expert riverman. For almost 100 years seagoing ships have reached Iquitos, Peru's isolated jungle town, more than 2,000 miles (3,212 kilometers) up the Amazon River. During the nineteenth and early twentieth centuries when the jungle was exploited for its rubber, huge fortunes were made, and there was a great trade in luxury goods from Europe and the United States.

In the highlands Lake Titicaca was first navigated in the late nineteenth century. In 1872 a steamship was brought from England, carried through the mountains in pieces on muleback to the lake, and then reassembled on the shore. It was used to carry passengers and cargoes of minerals between Peru and Bolivia. More steamers arrived, but these were later replaced by some modern cargo vessels. Tourists also travel by hydrofoil. Ecuador and Peru have their own small shipping fleets for international trade. Oceangoing ships and oil tankers also visit the coastal ports regularly.

The media
Every form of modern media is used in the Andean republics. In addition to radio, television, and video, there are newspapers,

magazines, telephones, telex, and fax machines.

Radio and television have a variety of state-owned and private channels. The most popular programs are films brought in from Europe and the United States, but a number of local movie companies produce their own. A few channels are run by religious or university groups, with an emphasis on education and culture.

Each country has its own national and provincial newspapers although circulation is restricted because of transportation difficulties. Magazines are published covering many topics from hobbies to political news. Comics are also popular. Although some newspapers date back to the beginning of this century, their publication has been stopped at times by government censorship. Today the three countries all enjoy freedom of the press.

It is possible to dial direct by telephone to most cities. Because the cost of an individual telephone is very high, most people use the state-run public facilities. Even in the smallest villages there is usually a public telephone, or *cabina*, but a long-distance connection can mean a very long wait. In La Paz the chola street traders have found a way to link into the system, and they offer the same service from a telephone in their stalls.

9

Struggling Economies

In 1973 political events in the Middle East led to a dramatic increase in the price of oil. This was good news because oil had been discovered in the Oriente regions and the countries were able to export at high prices. It was bad news because, as a result of the increased oil price, United States and European banks found they had a surplus of dollars. Looking for places to invest the dollars, the banks loaned billions of them to many Latin American countries. The Andean countries invested their loans in new industrial and commercial projects and began to enjoy a degree of prosperity. A few years later, however, it became obvious that the Latin American countries were unable to keep up with the repayment of these loans, and the decade of the 1980s was a continual economic struggle. World prices fell for some of the Andean countries' major exports while, at the same time, they needed to import many essential commodities from other countries. The resulting balance of payments did not leave the countries with enough money to pay off their debts, and the people of Ecuador, Peru, and Bolivia have experienced severe unemployment and inflation.

Oil and gas

When oil was discovered in Ecuador's Oriente region in 1967, it seemed that the country's fortune had changed. Within a few years oil accounted for nearly 70 percent of the country's export earnings. The oil was exploited by companies such as Texaco and Gulf Oil. A pipeline, 309 miles (499 kilometers) long, was built to carry the oil from the Amazon lowlands, over the Andes, to Esmeraldas on the Pacific coast. The situation changed drastically, however, when the world price of oil dropped, and in 1987 Ecuador suffered a devastating earthquake that broke the pipeline. Production was halted for almost six months, and the loss of sales, combined with the cost of repairs, deprived the country of almost half of its national budget. As a member of OPEC, Ecuador increased its oil production during the troubles of the early 1990s in the Middle East. Today, oil is also of great importance to Peru's economy. Most of the deposits are in the jungle regions near the borders with Ecuador, Colombia, and Brazil. Although Bolivia, too, has oil deposits, natural gas reserves are economically more important.

Mining and manufacturing

Traditionally, minerals have been the main exports of Bolivia and Peru. Since the collapse of the world tin price, Bolivia has mined only small amounts of tin, but it is the world's leading producer of antimony and a major producer of tungsten. Other minerals extracted include gold, iron ore, silver, zinc, lead, and copper. In Peru the most important minerals are copper, silver, lead, zinc, gold, and iron ore. Few minerals have been exploited in Ecuador.

Manufacturing industries face the same

problems in all three countries. They suffer from shortages of raw materials, skilled labor, and money for investment. Also, only a small number of people in each country are able to buy the products that it manufactures. In Ecuador most of the industries are around Quito and Guayaquil, and in Peru they are around Lima and the port of Callao. Both countries produce foods, textiles, household goods, metal and paper products, cement, and plastics. Peru also has car-assembly plants and a shipbuilding industry.

Many parts of the Andes are rich in minerals, and mining is a traditional industry. At La Oroya in Peru, the smelter of CENTROMIN is used to produce metals including zinc and silver.

Farming and fishing

A large proportion of the population in all three countries is involved in agriculture. Much of this agriculture is subsistence farming, where small farmers grow enough for their own needs. They

lack the money for fertilizer, irrigation, and machinery to make the land commercially productive. The eastern Andean slopes and Oriente region are rich zones for a variety of tropical fruit, rice, coffee, and sugarcane, which are cultivated largely for local consumption. Brazil nuts are exported from the extensive rain forests, where there are also valuable hardwood trees suitable for the timber and furniture trade. The lack of transportation and facilities in the region, however, means that this resource cannot be fully exploited.

The coastal zones of Ecuador and Peru are agriculturally the most productive. In Ecuador bananas, cacao, from which we get cocoa and chocolate, coffee, sugarcane, and cotton are the most important crops. Sugarcane, cotton, rice, and fruit are grown in the valleys of coastal Peru.

Beef cattle are raised in the eastern lowlands, and small farmers keep cattle for milk or meat although the pasture is poor. Some sheep are raised in the highlands, and goats are raised on the coast.

In the 1960s Peru was the world's foremost fish meal producer. Millions of tons of anchovies were caught each year, but climatic factors and overfishing reduced the catch. For years the fishing fleets have often been idle. Shrimp and tuna are also exported by Ecuador.

The drug trade
The eastern slopes of the Andes in Peru and Bolivia are the world's major growing areas for the coca leaf. The Indians have grown the leaf for their own use for centuries. World demand for the

Cotton is one of the most important crops in the desert oasis valleys of southern Peru. Workers of a cotton cooperative collect the harvest.

drug, however, has led to large-scale cultivation, particularly in remote areas, where government authorities have the greatest difficulty controlling it. The drug barons who control the business have made huge fortunes. Small farmers, too, find they make more money from growing coca than from legal crops. Coca grows easily, needs little attention, and produces four crops a year. It is estimated that 60 percent of working Bolivians benefit in some way from the drug traffic. No one can be sure quite how much money is involved, but enough is returned and deposited in Bolivia's banks to help the balance of payments and the Bolivian economy. Attempts by foreign governments to help local military to stamp out the trade have not been successful. In some regions drug barons buy the allegiance of the local communities by building schools and hospitals.

Tourism

One of South America's main tourist attractions is in Peru. Not far from Cuzco, in a magnificent setting high on a forested mountain slope, is Machu Picchu, the so-called "Lost City of the Incas." Cuzco, with its fine churches, Incan walls, and surrounding Incan fortresses and ruins, is itself an important tourist center. Lake Titicaca, Indian life, Spanish colonial churches, ancient sites, the jungle, and the "bird islands" off the coast are all attractions that visitors from the United States and Europe enjoy. In recent years, however, the tourist industry in Peru has suffered because of the activities of the Shining Path

The leaves of the native coca plant have been used by Andean Indians for 2,000 years or more to help combat cold and hunger. Coca leaves are still sold legally for Indian use in the markets of Bolivia and Peru.

terrorists. Certain areas of the country are unsafe for international and even local tourists.

Off the coast of Ecuador, the Galapagos Islands are of particular interest to naturalists, but the number of visitors is controlled so that the wildlife is not disturbed. Tourism is an important industry because it brings in much-needed U.S. dollars and other foreign currency, so all three countries are eager to promote it.

The future

The social and economic problems in Ecuador, Peru, and Bolivia are formidable. Foreign governments, including the United States, and the group of Western European nations known as the European Community, recognize this and are providing financial and technical assistance. The American Peace Corps and British and European volunteers have been working with communities and in schools for many years. Missionary groups and international organizations, such as UNICEF and the World Health Organization, contribute toward education and health care. However, recent Shining Path terroristic attacks have caused many foreign aid programs to withdraw their workers from Peru. The United Nations, funded by foreign governments, the World Bank, and the International Development Bank, gives emergency aid. More people are receiving education than ever before, and there is a desire for progress. All three countries have now been politically stable for several years, and the hope must be that their governments will find a way of developing their considerable resources for the benefit of all their people.

Index

© Heinemann Children's Reference 1991
This edition originally published 1991 by
Heinemann Children's Reference, a division
of Heinemann Educational Books, Ltd.

369711S

Westlake Middle School
Media Center
2800 West 135th Avenue
Broomfield, CO 80020